HBJ SOCIAL STUDIES

FAMILIES

Titles in this series:

HBJ SOCIAL STUDIES
FAMILIES

HBJ **HARCOURT BRACE JOVANOVICH, PUBLISHERS**
Orlando   New York   Chicago   Atlanta   Dallas

CLASSROOM CONSULTANTS

JUDITH BERG
Bamber Valley Elementary School
Rochester, Minnesota

KAREN BRASCH
Ellsworth Elementary School
Vancouver, Washington

MARY BRIGMAN
Oakland Elementary School
Charleston, South Carolina

SALLY BROWN
Central School
Glen Rock, New Jersey

DELORES H. CASEY
#2 Benjamin Harrison School
Indianapolis, Indiana

MRS. VALERIE CHEVALIER
Beekman Elementary School
Poughquag, New York

JO ANN CHURCH
College Park School
Wilmington, North Carolina

JENNIFER JENKINS COOLEY
Taylorsville Elementary
Taylorsville, Mississippi

THRESEA A. COURTNEY
Austin Independent School District
Austin, Texas

ANNA M. FLORES
Lamar Elementary School
Corpus Christi, Texas

SAMUEL FRAZER
Baylis Elementary School
Syosset, New York

HELEN HOWLAND
Irving School
Duncan, Oklahoma

JUNKO KAKO
John Swett Elementary School
Oakland, California

SANDRA LEVENSON, Ed.S.
Stephen Foster Elementary School
Fort Lauderdale, Florida

DIANE LOUGHLIN
Antioch C. C. School District 34
Antioch, Illinois

EMILIE PAILLE
Arbor Station Elementary School
Douglasville, Georgia

KAREN ANN RICKETTS
Crouse Elementary School
Flushing, Michigan

KATHY G. WALKER
Highland Springs Elementary School
Highland Springs, Virginia

PEGGY WEGNER
Erie School
Elyria, Ohio

READABILITY

DR. JEANNE BARRY
Jeanne Barry and Associates, Inc.
Oakland, California

PHOTOGRAPH ACKNOWLEDGMENTS

KEY: T, Top; B, Bottom; L, Left; R, Right.

RESEARCH CREDITS: Photo Researchers, © George E. Jones III, 1979: 5TR. Photo Library, © R. Hamilton Smith, 1982: 5B. Peter Arnold Inc., © Ginger Chih: 53BL. The Image Works, © Mark Antman: 54. © Tom Tracy: 55TL, 75BL. © Betty Crowell: 75BR. © John Elk III, 1983: 91. After-Image, © Ron Dahlquist: 94BL. © Tom Tracy: 95B. Click, Chicago, © Brian Seed, 1982: 101T. Peter Arnold Inc., © Jacques Jangoux: 117T. Woodfin Camp, © Lauren Freudmann, 1981: 117BL. Magnum, © Bruno Barbey: 117BR. Peter Arnold Inc., © Stephanie Fitzgerald: 118BL. © National Film Board Phototeque of Canada: 118BR. © Enid Schildkrout: 119B. Photo Researchers, © Larry Mulvehill, 1981: 120TL. © Peter Menzel, 1980: 120BL. Magnum, © Bruno Barbey: 120BR. Contact, © Liu Heung Shing: 122B. © National Film Board Phototeque of Canada: 123L. Peter Arnold Inc., © Dieter Blum: 123R. (Continued on page 136.)

Printed in the United States of America

ISBN 0-15-373201-6

Table of Contents

Unit One

About You

Growing and Learning

How much have you grown?

Once you were a baby.
You had to **learn** many things.
You learned to talk.

You learned to walk.

Now you can do many different things.
Who helped you learn?

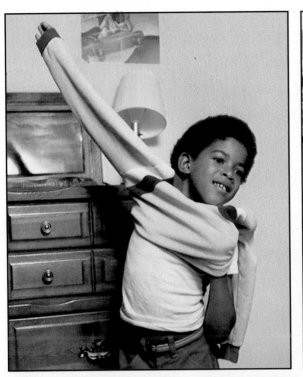

What other things have you learned?

2 Living with Other People

You learned to **share** with others.

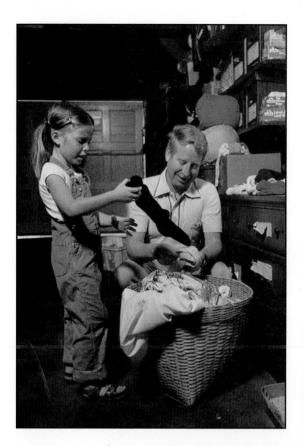

You learned to help others.

You learned to care for others.

3 Learning New Things

You are learning to do many things.
You are learning to count.

You are learning to write in **school.**

You are learning to read.
What other new things are you learning?

SKILLS PRACTICE

Alike and Different

These boxes are **alike.**

One box is **different.**

Which box is different?

How is it different?

How are these boxes different?

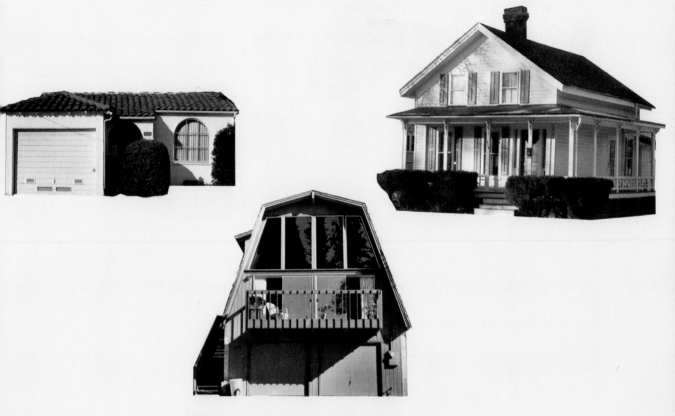

How are these houses alike?
How are they different?

SKILLS PRACTICE

What Is It Used For?

Look at these five things.
They are different in some ways.
How are they different?

These things are also alike in some ways.
They are used in games.
They are used for fun.
How else are they alike?

Here are four things that look different.

They are alike in some ways.

They are used in some of the same ways.

How are they used?

Now look at these three things.

How are they different?

How are they alike?

How do we use them?

What do we call them?

SKILLS PRACTICE

Where Is It?

Look at the picture. Then answer the questions.

1. The bookcase is to the right of the desk.
   What is to the left of the flag?

2. The wastebasket is in front of the
   desk. Who is behind the desk?

3. The bookcase is below the chalkboard.
   What is above the chalkboard?

4. Books are on the top shelf of the
   bookcase. What is on the bottom
   shelf?

5. The desk is between the teacher and the
   wastebasket. Is the door between the
   bookcase and the teacher?

Words to Remember

Match the words and the pictures.

1. grow
2. share
3. care
4. count
5. write
6. read

a.

b.

c.

d.

e.

f.

Ideas to Review

1. Once you were a baby. What are three ways you are different now?

2. What are three things your family helped you learn?

3. What are three things you are learning at school?

Skills Activities

1. Which things are alike? Which are different?

a.   b.   c.

2. Which things are used in the same way?

a.   b.   c.

3. Look at the picture. Then answer the questions.

    a. Is the car to the left of the house?

    b. Is the house behind the girl?

    c. Is the girl in front of the house?

    d. Is the kite below the boy?

    e. Is the dog between the boy and the girl?

Unit Two

About Families

Every Family Is Different

Some **families** are large.

Some families are smaller.

How many people are in these families?

2 Our Families Give Us Homes

We all need a place to live.

Families live in many different
kinds of homes.

3 Our Families Give Us Other Things We Need

Our families give us food.

Where do families get their food?

Our families give us the clothes we need.
We need many different kinds of clothes.
Where do we get our clothes?

Our families give us love, too.
How do families show love?

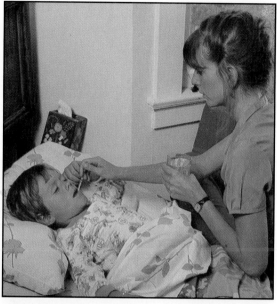

4 Families Work and Play Together

We share **work** with our families.

We help each other.

We learn from each other.
We learn new things together.

31

Families have fun together.

5 Families Have Rules

Rules tell us what we should do.
Rules also tell us what we should not do.
Every family has rules.
Different families have different rules.

Some rules teach us good table manners.

34

Some rules tell us when we can watch TV.

Some rules are about bedtime.

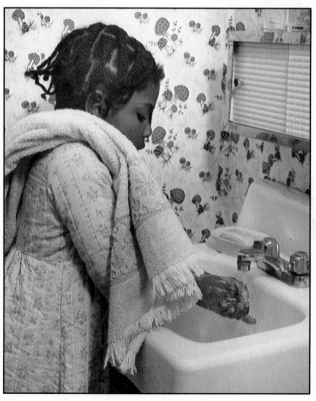

Families have rules about other people's things.

Families have rules about **safety.**

Families have rules about pets, too.

SKILLS PRACTICE

Comparing Views

This is a picture of Jeff's street.

Jeff is going into his house.

What else do you see in the picture?

This is also a picture of Jeff's street.
It shows how things look from above.
Find Jeff and his house.
What else can you find?

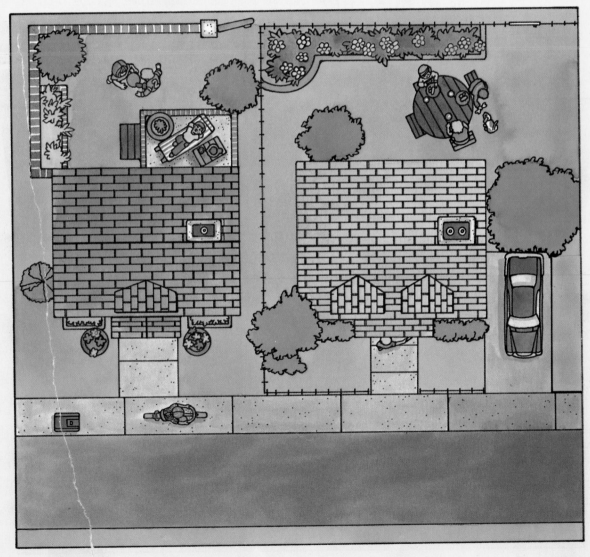

SKILLS PRACTICE

Understanding Maps and Symbols

This is a **map** of Jeff's street.

A map is a picture of a place.

How is the map like the picture on page 39?

How is it different?

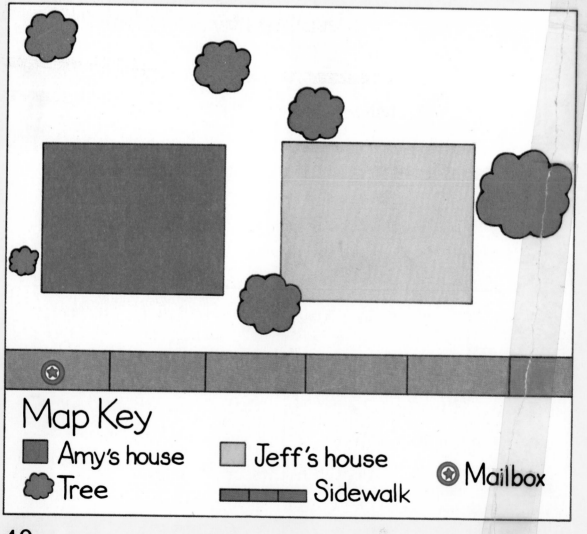

Map Key

Amy's house   Jeff's house   Mailbox

Tree   Sidewalk

Maps use **symbols.**

Symbols are small drawings of real things.

Symbols can be any shape or color.

Do these symbols look the same as the pictures?

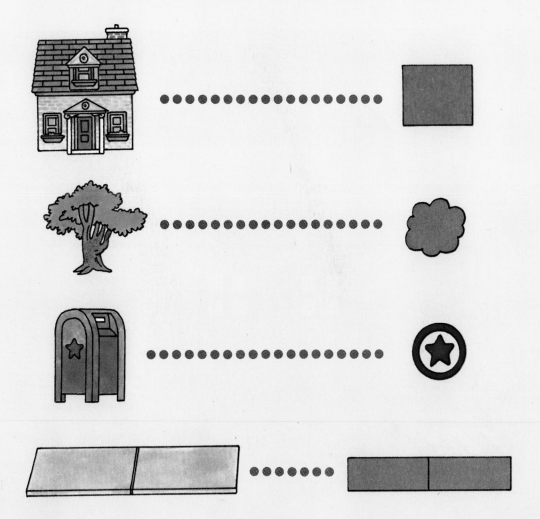

A **map key** tells what each symbol stands for.

Find the map key on the map.

On the map key, find the symbol for a tree.

How many trees are there on the map?

Now find the other symbols on the map.

SKILLS PRACTICE

Using a Map

Map Key

Store Tree Park

School House Road

Here is another map.

Look at the map and the map key.
Then answer the questions.

1. What is in the middle of the map?

2. How many houses are there?

3. How many stores are there?

4. What is between the school and the houses?

5. What is behind the school?

6. Which road is in front of the school?

Words to Remember

Match the words and the pictures.

1. family
2. rule
3. map
4. symbol
5. map key

a.

b.

c.

d.

e.

Ideas to Review

1. How are families different?

2. What are four things our families give us?

3. What are four things families do together?

4. What kinds of rules do families have?

44

Skills Activities

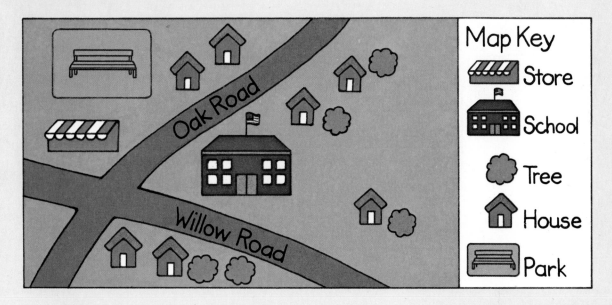

Look at the map and the map key.
Then answer the questions.

1. What is in the middle of the map?

2. How many stores are there?

3. What is between the park and the school?

4. What is behind the store?

More Activities

Draw a map of your classroom or your bedroom.
Draw a map key to go with it.

Unit Three

Needs and Wants

47

1 People Have Needs

Needs are things people must have.
Families need a place to live.
We need food to eat and water to drink.

We need clothes to keep us warm and dry.

Some clothes help keep us cool when it is hot.

What other needs do people have?

2 People Have Wants

Wants are things that people would like to have.

Families cannot always have everything
they want.
They must choose what they want most.

3 What Do People Buy?

People buy things they need and want.
They use **money** to pay for things.

Look at what this family is buying.
Which are needs?
Which are wants?

People spend money in different ways.
They buy things that will last a long time.
They buy things they really need.

They buy some things just for fun.
They buy things that will last a short time.

Working for What We Need and Want

People must **work** to earn money.
People use money to buy things.
People work in many different places.
They work inside and outside.

Some people work alone.

Many people work with other people.

People have many different kinds of jobs.
Sometimes their jobs help other people.
Jobs that help others are called **services.**
How are these people helping?

Some people make things.

Things people make are called **goods.**

What are these people making?

Children Work, Too

Sometimes children have jobs.
They work to buy the things they want.

What jobs do these young people have?

SKILLS PRACTICE

Making Lists

Why do we make lists?
Sometimes we make lists for fun.
We make lists of things we like.
Sometimes we need to remember things.
Lists help us remember.

Which things do not belong on these lists?

Things to buy at the grocery store
1. bread
2. a haircut
3. oranges
4. milk

Things I like to do
1. sing
2. swim
3. play ball
4. pencils

SKILLS PRACTICE

Which Are Needs
and Which Are Wants?

Needs are things that are important.
Needs are important for life and health.

Wants are things that are nice to have.
Wants are things we can live without.

Look at these two lists.

1. Which list shows needs?

2. Which list shows wants?

3. How would you finish these lists?

1. place to live	1. puzzle
2. food	2. roller skates
3. love	3. pony ride
4. [?]	4. [?]

SKILLS PRACTICE

People at Work

Who are these workers? What are they doing?

1.

2.

3.

4.

5.

6.

What do the workers need to do their jobs?

Match the workers with the things they use
   at work.

a.

b.

c.

d.

e.

f.

SKILLS PRACTICE

Reading a Map

Maps show where things are.
This is a map of a shopping center.
People buy things at shopping centers.

Look at the map. Then answer the questions.

1. Is the bookstore next to the parking lot?

2. Is the pet store next to the bookstore?

3. Which store is next to the toy store?

4. Which store is between the parking lot and the bookstore?

5. Which store is between the toy store and the grocery store?

UNIT 3 REVIEW

Words to Remember

Use these words to finish the sentences.

| money | wants | work | needs | buy |

1. _____ are things we cannot live without.

2. _____ are things we would like to have.

3. People _____ things they need and want.

4. People use _____ to pay for things.

5. People _____ to earn money.

Ideas to Review

1. What are three needs that all people have?

2. Name two services. What workers do these jobs?

3. Name two goods. What workers make these goods?

4. Name two jobs that children can have.

66

Skills Activities

Look at the pictures.

1. Make a list of the things that are needs.

2. Make a list of the things that are wants.

house   skates   milk   shoes

glove   flowers   paints   fruit

Look at the map. Then answer the questions.

1. Is the shoe store next to the bookstore?

2. Which store is next to the toy store?

3. Which store is between the toy store
   and the grocery store?

68

Unit Four

Changes All Around

Families Make Changes

Families **change.**

How are these families changing?

Seasons Bring Changes

Places change during the year.
Every **season** is different.
How is this farm changing?

Spring

Summer

Fall

Winter

Are the seasons different where you live?

3 Our Neighborhoods Change

Some **neighborhoods** do not stay the same.

People take down old buildings.

People build new buildings.

Sometimes old buildings are used in new ways.

Towns Change, Too

Towns do not always stay the same.
This is Rivertown long ago.

Rivertown changed into a **city.**

What changes do you see?

SKILLS PRACTICE

Day and Night

Look at the pictures. Then answer the questions.

1. Which things are happening in the morning?

2. Which things are happening in the afternoon?

3. Which things are happening at night?

a.

b.

c.

d.

e.

f.

SKILLS PRACTICE

What Time Is It?

Choose the right time.

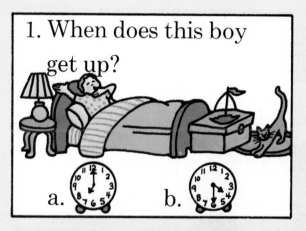

1. When does this boy get up?

a.   b.

2. When do these children eat lunch?

a.   b.

3. When do these children go home from school?

a. 9 30   b. 2 30

4. When does this family eat dinner?

a.   b. 6 00

Which clocks show the same time?

 1.    2.    3.    4.

SKILLS PRACTICE

The Days of the Week

There are seven days in a week.
Sunday is the first day.

Sunday	Monday	Tuesday	Wednesday	Thursday	Friday	Saturday
1	2	3	4	5	6	7
		I rode my bike.	Today I am playing baseball.	I will play soccer.		

Look at the pictures. Then answer the questions.

1. What is the last day of the week?

2. What day comes after Tuesday?

3. What day comes after Thursday?

4. What did Bob do on Tuesday?

5. What will Bob do on Thursday?

SKILLS PRACTICE

Past, Present, and Future

Things happening now are in the present.
Things that have already happened are
in the past.
Things that are going to happen are in
the future.

This is Ann in
the present.

Which pictures show Ann in the past?
Which pictures show Ann in the future?

1.   2.   3.   4.

SKILLS PRACTICE

Maps Can Show Changes

Maps can show how neighborhoods change.
This map shows Maria's neighborhood
   long ago.

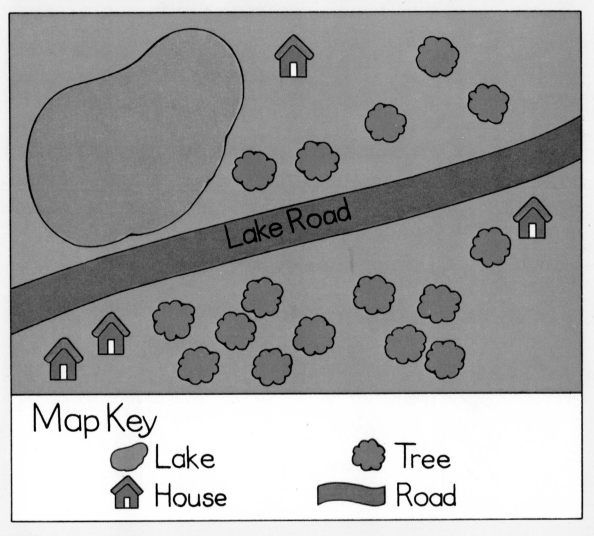

This map shows Maria's neighborhood today.
How has Maria's neighborhood changed?
How has it stayed the same?

Map Key

Lake

Tree

House

Store

School

Road

Lake Road

UNIT 4 REVIEW

Words to Remember

Match the words and the pictures.

1. change
2. seasons
3. neighborhood
4. city
5. week

a.   b.   c.

d.   e.

Ideas to Review

1. How do families change? Name two ways.

2. What are the four seasons?

3. How are the seasons different where you live?

4. How do neighborhoods change? Name two ways.

5. How do towns change?

Skills Activities

What time is it? How can you tell?

1.

2.

3.

What day comes next?

1. Monday
   Tuesday
   [?]

2. Wednesday
   Thursday
   [?]

3. Friday
   Saturday
   [?]

More Activities

1. Draw a picture. Show two things you do during the day. Write the times on your picture.

2. What do you want to do in the future? Tell about something you want to learn.

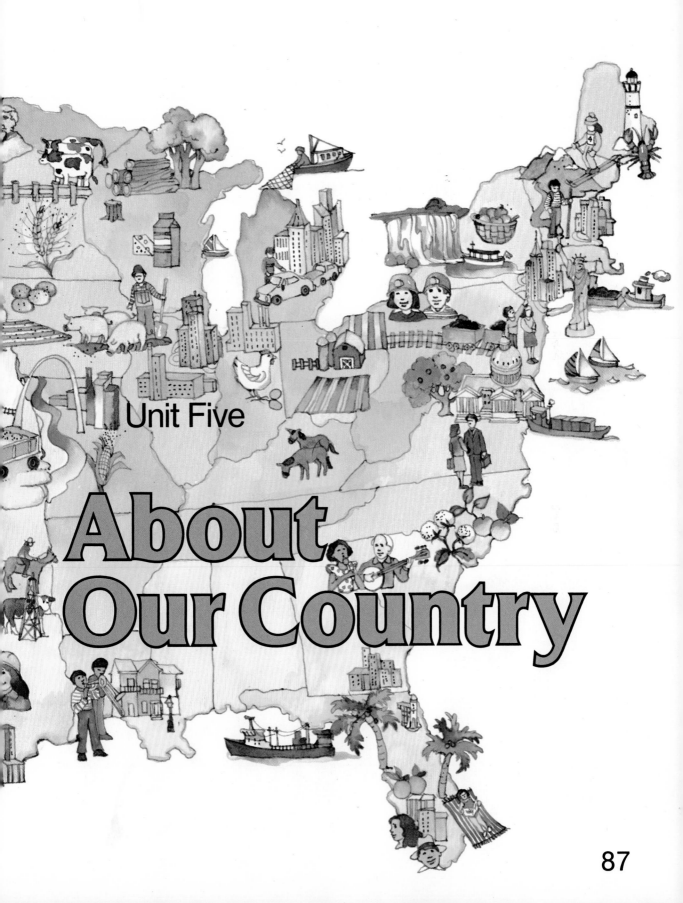

Unit Five

About Our Country

The American People

We are all **Americans.**

We live in the **United States of America.**

Americans are different in many ways.
Americans are alike in many ways, too.

2 The United States

The United States is a big country.

Our country has many beautiful places.
We work to keep these places clean.
We try to keep them beautiful.

The United States has many big cities.

Many, many Americans live in these cities.

Other Americans live in small towns.

Other Americans live on **farms.**
They grow the food that we all need.

3 Our Country's Resources

Our country has many **resources.**
Resources are things that people use.

Trees and water are resources.

Oil and land are resources, too.

Resources are used to
make things we need.

We must use our resources
carefully.
We want them to last a
long time.

4 Our Country's Past

Indians were the first Americans.
They lived in all parts of the United States.
They lived in many kinds of homes.

In 1492 Christopher Columbus came to America.
He told people about the land he had found.
Soon, other people came to America.

This picture shows the Pilgrims.
They came to America long ago.
Their first year was hard.
The Indians helped them.
The Indians and the Pilgrims
    shared a big dinner.
It was the first Thanksgiving.

Other people came to America.

They came from many different countries.

They sailed across the ocean in small ships.

They built houses.

They planted **crops.**

They worked hard in their new country.

5 Remembering Our Country's Past

The United States once belonged to a
country called England.
Americans wanted to be free.
They fought to have their own country.
We **celebrate** this on Independence Day.
It is our country's birthday.

On Independence Day we honor our **flag.**

It stands for the United States.

We honor our flag on many other days, too.

Remembering Our Country's Leaders

Many people have helped our country. We remember these people on their birthdays.

George Washington was our first **President.**
He fought for our country's freedom.
His birthday is on February 22.

Abraham Lincoln was a President, too.
He kept our country together.
He helped all Americans become free.
His birthday is on February 12.

Long ago, women could not vote.
Susan B. Anthony helped change
    that.
Today, all Americans can vote.
February 15 is Susan B. Anthony
    Day.

This is a picture of Martin
    Luther King, Jr.
He helped change our country.
He helped make it more fair.
We honor Martin Luther King
    on January 15.

103

SKILLS PRACTICE

Living and Working Together

People belong to many **groups.**

These people are in the same family.

These children go to the same school.

These children live in the same neighborhood.

We all live in the same country.

How can we be good group members?

We follow rules.

We share.

We help each other.

We listen.

We are polite.

We work together.

SKILLS PRACTICE

Our Families

Look at these people.
How are they being good family members?

SKILLS PRACTICE

Our School

How can we be good members of our school?

We follow the rules.

How are these children being good school members?

SKILLS PRACTICE

Our Neighborhoods

We must all be good neighbors.

How are these people being good neighbors?

SKILLS PRACTICE

Our Country

How can we be good Americans?

We keep our country clean.

We learn about our country.   We obey its rules.

How else can we be good Americans?

SKILLS PRACTICE

A Map of the United States

UNITED STATES
OF AMERICA

CANADA

WASHINGTON

MONTANA

OREGON

IDAHO

WYOMING

PACIFIC
OCEAN

NEVADA

UTAH

COLORADO

CALIFORNIA

PACIFIC
OCEAN

HAWAII

ARIZONA

NEW MEXICO

ALASKA

CANADA

MEXICO

PACIFIC OCEAN

Maps can show very big places.

This is a map of the United States.

It shows the 50 parts of our country.

Each part is called a **state.**

Can you find your state on the map?

Words to Remember

Use these words to finish the sentences.

crops	Independence Day	groups
resource	Thanksgiving	

1. Trees are a ____.

2. The Pilgrims and Indians had the first ____.

3. Farmers plant ____.

4. We celebrate our country's freedom on ____.

5. We all belong to many ____.

Ideas to Review

1. Who were the first Americans?

2. Who were the Pilgrims?

3. What does our flag stand for?

4. Who was our first President?

Skills Activities

Match the sentences and the pictures.

1. We listen and are polite.

2. We put things away.

3. We keep our country clean.

4. We take turns.

5. We help each other.

6. We learn about our country.

a.

b.

c.

d.

e.

f.

More Activities

1. List three of the rules in your school.

2. Look at the map of our country on pages 110 and 111. Find your state. Name a state that is next to your state. Name a state that is far from your state.

114

Unit Six

A Look at the World

Our Country and the World

The United States is our country.

There are many countries in the **world.**

Every country is different.

No two countries look alike.

No two countries have the same past.

The people of every country are different, too.
They have their own ways of doing things.

Mexico

China

Nigeria

How Are People Alike?

Families all over the world have the same needs.
We all need homes to live in.

Nigeria

Mexico

China

Canada

China

Canada

We all need food.

We all need clothes.

We all need love from our families and friends.

Nigeria

We must work to get the things we need.
People all over the world do many of the
same jobs.
What are these people doing?

China

Canada

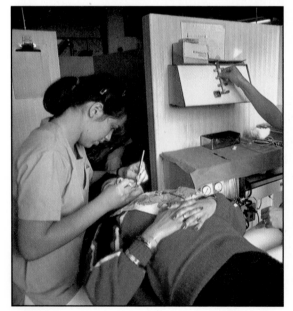

Mexico

Nigeria

3 The Changing World

The world is always changing.
People change the land.
People use resources.
Cities grow larger.

Canada

China

People learn new ways of doing things.
They share what they know.

Nigeria

China

Just like you, people everywhere grow
and change.

4 Holidays Around the World

Canada

Nigeria

People all over the world have **holidays.**

Holidays are times for sharing fun.

China

In China, Spring Festival is an
important holiday.
Spring Festival begins the new year
in China.
People go to parades.
Everyone wishes for good luck in the new year.

Mexico once belonged to a country called Spain.
Today Mexico is a free country.
Mexicans celebrate their Independence Day
   in September.

Mexico

At night they watch fireworks.
The next day they have parties and parades.
How is their Independence Day like ours?

SKILLS PRACTICE

What Is a Globe?

A **model** is a small copy of something.
Picture 1 shows a model of an airplane.
Picture 2 shows a real airplane.
Which other pictures show models?

1.

2.

3.

4.

5.

6.

This is a picture of the **Earth.**

The girl is looking at a **globe.**
A globe is a small model of the Earth.
The globe is the same shape as the Earth.
What shape is it?

SKILLS PRACTICE

What Globes Show

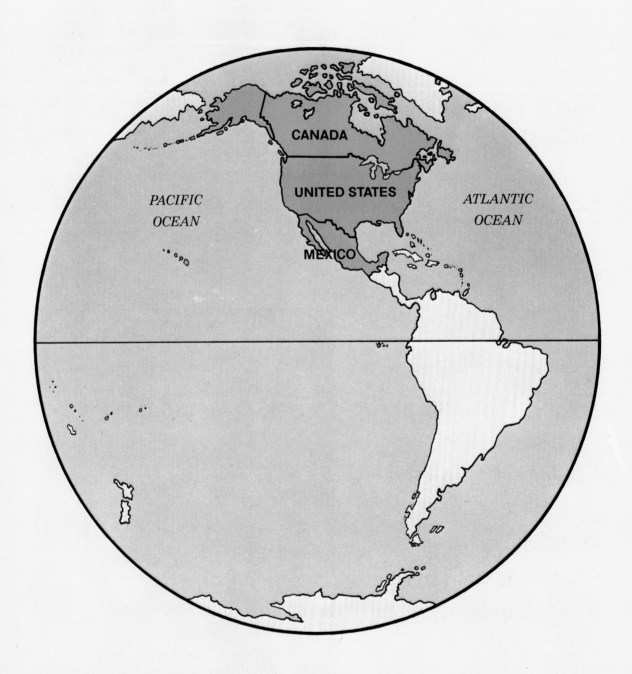

Globes show land and water.
Land is many different colors.
What color is water?

Look at the globe. Then answer the questions.

1. Find the Atlantic Ocean. What other
    ocean can you find?

2. Find the United States. What other
    countries can you find?

SKILLS PRACTICE

Learning About Directions

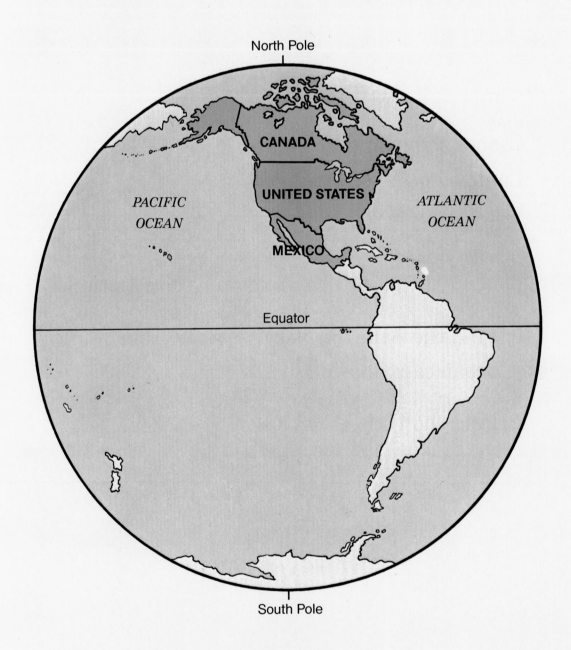

North Pole

CANADA

UNITED STATES

PACIFIC
OCEAN

ATLANTIC
OCEAN

MEXICO

Equator

South Pole

Globes show more than land and water.

Globes show the **North Pole** and the **South Pole.**

Globes also show the **equator.**
The equator is a make-believe line.
It runs all around the globe.

Find the equator on the globe.
Find the North Pole.
Put your finger on the equator.
Now move your finger toward the North Pole.
You are moving north.

Find the South Pole.
Put your finger on the equator.
Now move your finger toward the South Pole.
You are moving south.

Is Canada north or south of the United States?
Is Mexico north or south of the United States?

Words to Remember

Match the words and the pictures.

1. world
2. holiday
3. model
4. globe
5. equator

a.

b.

c.

d.

e.

Ideas to Review

1. In what ways are the people of the world alike?

2. What do people do on holidays?

3. What is an important holiday in China?

4. What is an important holiday in Mexico?

Skills Activities

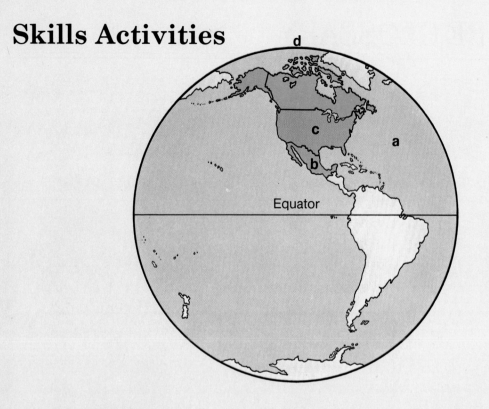

Look at the globe. Then answer the questions.

1. What letter is on the United States?

2. What letter is on the North Pole?

3. What letter is on Mexico?

4. What letter is on the Atlantic Ocean?

More Activities

Look at a globe. Name the country that is north of the United States. Name two countries that are south of Canada.

PICTURE GLOSSARY

alike (p. 12)

celebrate (p. 100)

change (p. 70)

city (p. 77)

crops (p. 99)

different (p. 12)

Earth (p. 127)

equator (p. 131)

family (p. 22)

farm (p. 93)

flag (p. 101)

globe (p. 127)

goods (p. 57)

group (p. 104)

holiday (p. 123)

learn (p. 3)

list (p. 60)

map (p. 40)

House Tree School map key (p. 41)	model (p. 126)	money (p. 52)
needs (p. 48)	neighborhood (p. 74)	resources (p. 94)
rule (p. 34)	safety (p. 37)	school (p. 10)
seasons (p. 72)	service (p. 56)	share (p. 6)
state (p. 111)	symbol (p. 41)	town (p. 76)
United States (p. 88)	wants (p. 50)	work (p. 30)

PHOTOGRAPH ACKNOWLEDGMENTS

KEY: T, Top; B, Bottom; L, Left; C, Center; R, Right.

HBJ PHOTOS: 13BR, 89TL, 105TR, 105BR.

HBJ PHOTOS by Erik Arnesen: 15CR, 59BL, 105TL.

HBJ PHOTO by Edward Barnett: 71T.

HBJ PHOTOS by Josephine Coatsworth: 9, 56TR.

HBJ PHOTOS by Rick Der: 12, 13T, 14, 15B.

HBJ PHOTO by Dan DeWilde: 95T.

HBJ PHOTOS by Alec Duncan: 2, 3, 4, 5, 6, 7, 8, 10, 11, 15T, 15CL, 22, 23, 24, 26, 27, 28, 29, 30, 31TL, 31B, 34, 35, 36, 37, 48, 49, 50, 51, 52, 53T, 53BR, 55TR, 56TL, 56BL, 57TL, 58, 59T, 59BR, 70, 71BR, 74, 88, 89TR, 89CR, 89B, 104T, 104BL, 105C, 105BL, 106, 107, 108, 116, 126, 127B.

HBJ PHOTO by Elaine F. Keenan: 13BC.

HBJ PHOTO by Susan Lohwasser: 89CL.

HBJ PHOTO by Norman Prince: 32T.

HBJ PHOTO by Karen Rantzman: 13BL.

HBJ PHOTO by Elliot Varner Smith: 101B.

HBJ PHOTO by Tom Tracy: 104BR.

HBJ PHOTOS by Frank Wing: 31TR, 119TR, 120TR.

RESEARCH CREDITS: Stock, Boston, William Finch: 25TL. Sygma, Mickey Pfleger: 32B. Cameramann International, Milt and Joan Mann: 55B. San Francisco Fire Department, Chet Born: 56BR. Stock, Boston, Cary Wolinsky: 57TR, 57BL. Courtesy Stride Rite Corporation, 5 Cambridge Center, Cambridge Massachusetts 02142: 57BR. After-Image, Steve Vidler: 70BL. Stock, Boston, J. R. Holland: 75T. Stock, Boston, Peter Simon: 91T. National Park Service, L. Kirk: 91BL. Grant Heilman Photography, Alan Pitcairn: 91BR. Grant Heilman: 92. Taurus Photos, William R. Wright: 93T. United States Department of Agriculture: 93B. Boise Cascade: 94TL. Tennessee Valley Authority: 94TR. Stock, Boston, Daniel Brody: 94BR. Black Star, David Moore: 100. New York Historical Society, *George Washington* by Charles Wilson Peale: 102T. New York Historical Society, *Abraham Lincoln* by William E. Marshall: 102B. Library of Congress: 103T. Black Star, C. Ray Moore: 103B. Stock, Boston, Frank Sitemen: 109T. Photo Library, Anne Griffiths: 109BL. After-Image, David Falconer: 109BR. Photri: 118TL. Stock, Boston, Owen Franken: 118TR. Stock, Boston, Richard Balzer: 119TL. Cameramann International, Milt and Joan Mann: 121L. Stock, Boston, Richard Balzer: 121R. Photri: 122T. China Pictorial Magazine: 124. After-Image, Moldvay: 125. NASA: 127T.

ART ACKNOWLEDGMENTS

Rosemary Deasy: 16, 18, 19, 44, 62, 63, 67T, 78, 79, 80, 81, 84, 85, 113, 132. Terry Hoff: 96, 97, 98, 99. Intergraphics: 38, 39, 40, 41, 42, 45, 64, 67B, 82, 83, 128, 130, 133. Christa Kieffer: 72, 73, 76, 77. Susan Lexa: 1, 20–21, 46–47, 68–69, 86–87, 114–115.

MAP CREDITS

R. R. Donnelley Cartographic Services: 110–111.

COVER CREDIT

HBJ PHOTO by Alec Duncan

A 4
B 5
C 6
D 7
E 8
F 9
G 0
H 1
I 2
J 3